Verses From
South West England

Edited by Michelle Afford

 Young**Writers**

First published in Great Britain in 2007 by:
Young Writers
Remus House
Coltsfoot Drive
Peterborough
PE2 9JX
Telephone: 01733 890066
Website: www.youngwriters.co.uk

SB ISBN 978-1 84431 130 9

Foreword

Young Writers was established in 1991 and has been passionately devoted to the promotion of reading and writing in children and young adults ever since. The quest continues today. Young Writers remains as committed to the nurturing of poetic and literary talent as ever.

This year's Young Writers competition has proven as vibrant and dynamic as ever and we are delighted to present a showcase of the best poetry from across the UK and in some cases overseas. Each poem has been selected from a wealth of *Little Laureates* entries before ultimately being published in this, our sixteenth primary school poetry series.

Once again, we have been supremely impressed by the overall quality of the entries we have received. The imagination, energy and creativity which has gone into each young writer's entry made choosing the poems a challenging and often difficult but ultimately hugely rewarding task - the general high standard of the work submitted ensured this opportunity to bring their poetry to a larger appreciative audience.

We sincerely hope you are pleased with this final collection and that you will enjoy *Little Laureates Verses From South West England* for many years to come.

Contents

Hillcrest Primary School, Totterdown

Kea Community Primary School, Truro

Phoebe Maggs (10)	30
Hannah Susnjara (10)	30
Henry Eades (9)	31
Jade Whalley (10)	31
Eddie Coombs (10)	32
Joe D'Souza (10)	32
Josh Neal (10)	32
Lucy Topham (9)	33
Quincy Smith (9)	33
Catherine Marston (9)	34
Sam Adams (9)	34
Jordan Gaslonde (10)	35
Beth Richards (8)	35
James Spencer (7)	36
William House (10)	36
Christopher Marshall (11)	36
Felicity Freeborn (8)	37
Susannah Johnston (8)	37
Katie Brown (7)	38
Isabel Wellings (7)	38
Tom Knuckey (8)	39
Tom Praed-Mather (8)	39
Imogen Robson (7)	39
Rachel Addey (9)	40
Phoebe Staines (7)	40
Daisy Cochran Scarratt (9)	41
Davinia Davey (9)	41
Anna Gowenlock (8)	42
Katie Croft-Hill (8)	42
Lily Sullivan (8)	43
Will Drury (10)	43
Lauren Thompson (10)	44
Edward Jose (11)	44

St Mary's Primary School, Bridgwater

Thomas Roles (10)	45
Ryan Deans (10)	45
Luke Dyer (10)	46
Luke Payne (11)	47
Courtney Boobyer (10)	48
Austin Hodges (11)	48

Jacob Sidebotham (10)   49
Jake Gardener (10)   49
Courtney Barrow (10)   50
Jessica Dunn (10)   50
Charlie Fletcher (10)   51
Wesley Williams (11)   51
Zoe Rowe (10)   52
Luke Shaw (10)   52
Sarah Mansell (11)   53
Amy Scriven (10)   53
Jayden Parr (10)   54
Fern Thompson (11)   55
Tom Rich (10)   56
Emily Frost (11)   57
Jack Tottle (11)   58
Sophie Jordan (11)   58
James Lloyd (10)   59
Bradley Warren (10)   59
Sophie Manship (11)   60
Edward Page-Symonds (11)   60
Laura Hallett (10)   61
Olivia Tucker (10)   62

St Philip's CE Primary School, Bath

Jess Walter (9)   62
Maisie Skuse (10)   63
Jessica Blackwell (9)   64
Georgia Symonds (9)   64
Cameron Davies (9)   65
Olivia Simms (9)   65
Alyx Ball (9)   66
Nadia Bancroft   66
Olivia Parkyn (8)   67
Victoria Horroll (9)   67
Yazmin Moss (8)   68
Sophie Clark (8)   68
Hannah Hewett (7)   68
Cobi Short (8)   69
Tyra Smith (9)   69
Libby Walter (7)   69
Abi Brewer (7)   70

Maddie McCarthy (8)   70
Aimee Huntley (7)   70
George Godwin (8)   71
Ria Beeho (8)   71
Jacob Quintin (8)   71
Brandon Morrison (9)   72
Ben Bradley (8)   72
Tallon Leach (8)   73
Charlotte Marsh (8)   73
Thomas Fowden (7)   73
Jess Szafran (8)   74
Brioney Evans (8)   74
Sadie Moyle (8)   74
Carla Ferris (8)   75
Curtis Gay (9)   75
Nick Atwell (8)   75
Lucy Cryer (7)   76
Akhilesh Pai (9)   76
Karli-Anne Lunt (8)   77
Sam Woodham (8)   77
Jessica Bush (9)   78
Wilson Skyrme (8)   78
Ellen Ascott (8)   78

St Thomas a Becket School, Tilshead

Isabel Smith (9)   79
Kiera O'Neill (10)   79
Tara Skinner (10)   80
Chloe Jackson (9)   80
Oliver Cogbill (9)   81
Ricky Lawrence (9)   81
Kyra Player (9)   82
Harriet Shakerley (10)   82
Iona Wilkinson (9)   83
Daniel Evans (10)   83
David Martin (10)   84
Jake Atfield (9)   84
Ruby Withers (11)   85
Bradley Kinsey (11)   86
Emily Withers (8)   86
Jessica Vincent (10)   87

Reuben Wright (9)   87
George Smith (10)   88
Emma Miller (10)   88
Luke Haggaty (8)   89

West Coker Primary School, Yeovil
Chiara Thiella (7)   89
Lucy Manly (7)   90
Josh Boon (9)   90
Nea Graziano (8)   91
Emily Andrews (8)   91
Kim Centamore (9)   92
Bran Pick (10)   92
Charlie Cowley (8)   93
Francesca Graziano (10)   93
Charlotte Taylor (8)   94
Victoria White (9)   94
Danny Gilham (8)   95
Molly Morris (10)   95
Sophie Pinkett (8)   96
Joshua Cresswell (8)   96
Henry Morris (8)   97
Otis Pick (8)   97
Sammy Hubbard (7)   98
Jenny Taylor (10)   98
Megan Manly (9)   98
Jake Symes (9)   99
Bethany Hubbard (10)   99
Jemma Reddaway (10)   99

The Poems

Fall In Love With A World Of Amazement

This world of beauty and nature
A wild fantasy
Just look around the corner
And maybe you will see
Life is full of surprises and beauty
From frosty winters
To amazing sunsets
And wonderful colours
This is as good as life gets
What else could you need?
Get trapped in harmony's spell
Fall in love with views of desire
The sweet scent of nature
The amazing smell
This world of beauty and nature
A wild fantasy
Just look around the corner
And maybe you will see
Life is full of amazement and beauty.

Alicia Peacock (10)

The Blanket Of Dreams

Fetch me thread from the sun
Fetch me thread from the moon
And the rest I shall get
Ideas from famous artists
Paint from Heaven
Then weave and sew and knit
Then there is the blanket of dreams.

Philippa Whitaker (7)
Bruton School for Girls, Bruton

Wolf

Mean growler
Old howler
Bone cruncher
Flesh muncher
Sheep teaser
Rabbit seizer
Creepy walker
Night stalker.

Ellie Parcell (8)
Hambridge Community Primary School, Hambridge

Wolf

Meat eater
Deep sleeper
Moonlight shrieker
Forest sneaker
Bone cruncher
Meat muncher
Sheep lover
Undercover.

Mahaela Wood (8)
Hambridge Community Primary School, Hambridge

Wolf

Sheep eater
Best creeper
Jaw cruncher
Rib muncher
Midnight howler
Forest prowler
Angry snarler
Scary growler.

Bill Brandt (8)
Hambridge Community Primary School, Hambridge

Fluffy The Mastiff

Slimy slobberer
Food gobbler
Has a pea-sized brain
Sometimes a pain
Big pooch
Looks like Hooch
Deep sleeper
Whiny weeper.

Daisy Cook (9)
Hambridge Community Primary School, Hambridge

Wolves

Sharp teeth
Eats beef
Grey growlers
Moonlight howlers
Slimy slobberers
Food gobblers
Proud walkers
Rabbit stalkers.

Lily Martin (9)
Hambridge Community Primary School, Hambridge

Wolf

Lamb chopper
Killed hopper
Night howler
Noon growler
Morning lurker
Eat the worker
Bone cruncher
Deer muncher.

Rosanna Strickland (8)
Hambridge Community Primary School, Hambridge

Gloom

Ghostly squirrels race up looming trunks
Till swallowed by the Mist Monster
And all that's heard of them is the muted shuffle of leaves
And the pitter-patter of small cascades of drips.

Vehicles driving out of the sea of gloom
Tractors looking like something from Star Wars
Car headlights like feelers on a bug
Drivers straining to see through the Mist Monster.

Abandoned cobwebs dangling from treetops to the ground
Dewdrops like pearls everywhere
Plants polished like wood, shining in the nearly-gone sun
No one wants to go out now, too cold
The land is deserted and is now a ghost town!

Harry Seal (10)
Hambridge Community Primary School, Hambridge

A Winter's Spell

Nature is brewing a misty potion
Stirring its wicked weather cauldron
Bubbling mists, cold and dew
Sprinkled all over the innocent land
Softly coating trees and houses
Conjuring them out of view.

This dreary, eerie, alien world
Is cloaked with pearly-white
Exchanging a dull blank canvas
For what was once a radiant sight.

Passing geese are like grey angels
Flying through thick air
Nodding their heads
And spreading their wings
Flying without a care.

Anna Carrington (10)
Hambridge Community Primary School, Hambridge

Mist Mayhem

As I stroll through this wood
I think I'm in a mist maze
And then I stop and gaze
At these beautiful pearls dancing on cobwebs
Doing their little jig in this mist mayhem!

As I walk through this wood
A drop of water falls off a tree and makes a ripple in a canal
Trees look like big black blobs in white land
A car comes through the mist and the fog lights look like lighthouses
A crowd of geese honk over the top of me
When I'm walking in this mist mayhem!

As I walk through this wood
Grass is covered with dew and rain
All land is covered with mist
If I look up all is mist and green huddling together to keep
in the warmth
On the floor footprints from horses have frosted over
When I walk on mud it crackles
As I'm walking in this mist mayhem!

As I'm nearly at the end of the wood
I'm going to say look out in case the mist is too thick
You might walk into a tree like I have!

Angus Lysaczenko (10)
Hambridge Community Primary School, Hambridge

Mist

Mist, you want to reach it
But it just disappears!

Mist is a white witch that creates a world of fears
Mist drapes shiny cobwebs upon a dripping tree
Mist floods the soggy land under its milky sea.

Mist makes a grey bay
Mist takes a sunny day then magics it away.

Zhanet Georgieva (10)
Hambridge Community Primary School, Hambridge

Foggy Lands

Shimmering grass sags in the mist land
Squirrels scamper off through foggy trees
Drips fall into puddles of nothing
Duckweed settles into astrofields
Willow trees brush each other swiftly
Gentle ripples open as drips fall in the winter winds.

Cobwebs dancing to their little jingle
Horse prints painted in the mud
Cats' eyes appearing in the mist
Horses walking in the jewelled grass.

Hedges disappearing into fields of nothing
Cows huddling to keep warm
Trees falling, rivers rushing in the winter rain
Sheep wool as thick as walls
Stingers stinging violently in the foggy land.

Leaves falling on the ground because the winter gusts of wind
Everything, all that is life, is dying out
Animals are hiding for the winter
Clouds are low and causing crashes
There's no hope for the animal kingdom
Life falls into darkness and so does the world
Mist getting lower, doesn't ever rise.

Adam Biswell (11)
Hambridge Community Primary School, Hambridge

Misty Day

Cats' eyes of cars peering through the winter's fog
Cautiously snaking through the spooky lanes
Passing the ends of tracks that lead to nowhere
Mist seeks through the window like a gas bomb
She shuts the window and gasps for breath
She passes a wood with squirrels scampering up the tree
She sees a cobweb swaying in the wind.

Edward Clark (10)
Hambridge Community Primary School, Hambridge

Bully

She's some scum, a goody-goody
She smells of garbage, I hate her
I want to get rid of her
But inside I can't
You can see she is sad and helpless
My gang wants to, they are raring to go
All I can do is call her stupid names
Everybody else is kicking and punching her
Giving her scars, scars on her body
And scars in her mind
I used to do that, I can't now
I feel as if I'm in her place
Being bullied by my mates
I wish I hadn't done it to start with
Then none of this would have happened.

Naomi Rowswell (9)
Hambridge Community Primary School, Hambridge

Misty Distance

Mobs of misty monsters
Come lurking through the grey
And the white witch of the west
Has made it a dismal day.

The daytime dawn is lost
In nature's steaming broth
But dawn's silence is broken
By the birds that have softly spoken.

The birds that have been speaking
Have been shot by the farmer shooting
And the cobweb that is dripping
A spider crawls shivering.

Rory Gauld (10)
Hambridge Community Primary School, Hambridge

Memories

Dancing, dangling cobwebs, a dewy dream
A jumping, jiggling jewel
The dripping decoration of a diamond necklace . . .
A shivering, stringy sparkle.

The day is still dozing under a duvet of mist
In this permanent doom-laden two-day of dusk
The day will not wake while the white witch's spell is here
Though trees try to tackle the mist with frayed-wire branches
They stand there frozen with fear.

A lonely bench stares out at nothing
Wrapped in sad old memories
It looks across the murky fields
Where school kids used to play
Now all that's left is a fat scruffy pigeon
Who's been pecking at worms all day.

A silent ghost stands alone
Shaking his head at the view
Nothing is left in this sad, sad world
Apart from mist and dew.

Sophie Brownhill (11)
Hambridge Community Primary School, Hambridge

The Road To Heaven

Down the lane to nowhere we go
Eyes wrapped in a grey blindfold of fog
Where a misted sign directs wandering lost souls
Through this alien heaven.

Somewhere a collie tenses her muscles
As she rounds her cattle into the ghastly mist
Tattered webs of soggy silk cling like vines to a tree
Their silvery baubles dancing a samba
Each droplet a stretching udder heavy with milk.

Matthew Cox (11)
Hambridge Community Primary School, Hambridge

A Black Cloak Of Darkness!

He silently creeps in
His thick black cloak covers all
Only the silvery moon is seen
Night has arrived at last.

Silently, sleepily River flows
Tired from day, she sleeps so still
Silvery reflections are seen inside her
Calmly she flows down the course.

Leaves and reeds blow gently
The wind breathes heavily as he sleeps
Softly, silently he moves through the trees
Sleeping high and low.

Suddenly an owl swoops down
Eyes fixed on a sleeping mouse
He makes no noise in flight
Gracefully swerving through the trees.

Everything is once more still
Calm and quiet, everything sleeps
The moon's silvery relaxing glow
Keeps everything asleep.

As silently as he came
His cloak is lifted up
Once more there is colour
Night has moved away.

Jessica Wiltshire (11)
Hambridge Community Primary School, Hambridge

A Winter's Day

As I walk I see glittery, silver-sparkled cobwebs
A house like a haunted manor
Cars like UFOs passing through smoke
A ghost bench perched alone
The white witch casts a spell
While a giant's hoary breath mists the world
The mist is a white dog running in shade
Trees like dark clouds on a hill.

The day having a lie in
Wind has stolen every life source
A gaggle of geese passes over like a storm of leaves
Headlights like guide dogs leading drivers through the misty maze
of lanes

A breeze softly stirs the grey
Tomorrow will never come
And water lies as still as a gravestone.

Overnight killers murdered colour
Lost, nothing moving, no noise, still
Little pearls on a spider's web
That dangles into nothingness
Blurry blotches are all that's there
Brambles bruised by the icy night.

Anne Gillard (11)
Hambridge Community Primary School, Hambridge

Wolf

Sheep eater
Best creeper
Jaw cruncher
Rib muncher
Midnight howler
Forest prowler
Angry snarler
Scary growler.

Shannon Wood (9)
Hambridge Community Primary School, Hambridge

Misty Darkness

Covered cobwebs drape the signpost
They cling and swing like thin lianas
Dancing a jig to the misty music
Weighed down by clear diamonds.

A misty pavement, a mysterious drive
Where a damp track vanishes
And mist fills a sleepy hollow
Thick and white as drifting snow.

A bench sits in the foggy darkness
With only grass to keep it happy
Staring into the paralysed world of mist
A world that's lost in sleep.

The white witch's spell is broken
The land awakes to sun and light
Forests and fields are full of colour
And all the world is bright!

Nicola Livingstone (11)
Hambridge Community Primary School, Hambridge

The Mist

The dark sky is overwhelmed by fog
The land is lost in silent daytime night
Mist erases the scene with its chilly hand
No sounds, no colours, no animals, no life.

Bushes' blurry shapes are sunk in the mind
A ghostly bench stands in a field alone
With only lifeless spirits for company
Where hedges merge in the mist as grey as bone.

The world fades down a mystery lane
Where the fog has become a grey-faced king
Trees loom suspiciously over the road
And rooks squawk, but no birds sing.

Rhudi Martin (11)
Hambridge Community Primary School, Hambridge

The Misty Land

A lonely bench sits in the cold, staring into nothingness.
The edge of the world.
It only sees a blurred-out line of what used to be there.
You can feel the sadness flowing out, as this misty blanket lays
on the earth
Life stays still and quiet as if it remains asleep.
The light of the world has been trapped, colour has been forgotten,
as has this world.
All over the levels, mist horses drift, covering everywhere
in the blankness of the fog.
This misty brew is bubbling up from river and moor, forest and bog.
Its steamy vapour rises like ghosts that haunt the land of Man.

Andrew Corns (10)
Hambridge Community Primary School, Hambridge

The Cliff

I know that he's watching me all the time
Whenever, wherever I go I can feel his eyes boring into me
I look and search, but I can't see him
Then he leaps, biting and ripping and tearing at me.

I go home bleeding, cold and shivering
When I sleep I hear monotonous creepy chanting
I wake up trembling and sweating again.

I dare not tell a single soul
What the bully does to me
Or what I'm going to do today
But I know what they'd say.

It's all my fault and I'll solve it now
Today it's the school trip and I know what to do
I'll go to the top of the cliff
I'll walk, then run, never looking behind, ignoring all
I'll jump and then . . . goodbye, cruel, cruel world!

Emily Allen (10)
Hambridge Community Primary School, Hambridge

Wind And Storm

As the storm walked closer
The wind whistled through the keyholes of the shivering houses
One stormy, strong, strange night.
The leaves rustled off the trees and followed the roaring wind
Whilst the darkness drowned the town
Backed up by evil, surrounding the town with nowhere to run or hide
Flash! the lightning had first struck, lit up the whole area
                                              as if it were day
Bang! as the thunder told the lightning to hit the city clock
And it did so
It hit the city clock . . . there was a long pause and,
Creak . . .
The tall helpless clock slowly made its way for a paddle in the river
And so they had the right to
Several scared screaming victims ran helplessly
As the evil grabbed them, never to see the light of day again
Hiding them from the world's joy, not to see a happy face ever again
As the clock slowly sank, it too downed all rowers in its path.

Jamie Finlayson (10)
Hazlegrove Preparatory School, Sparkford

Fire

The fire crept towards the trees
The grass yelled as it was scorched
Fire licked and roared
As it was prevented from entering the building
And destroying the people
A spark flew from the rock and hit the straw
A few seconds later the whole barn was on fire.

Milo Barran (11)
Hazlegrove Preparatory School, Sparkford

The Rugby Game

The grass screamed as the players tramped on it
The ball whistled as it flew through the air
The posts wobbled as the ball bounced off them
The stands exploded as a try was scored
The whistle shrieked for half-time.

Caspar Fish (11)
Hazlegrove Preparatory School, Sparkford

Storm

Whispering and wandering
Went the wind through the house
And people were asleep like a log.
Then the storm started
Creeping and crawling
And the mean storm
Jumped and jived on the furniture
Whirling and walloping.
All of the storm
Jumped on the house.
Then all of a sudden
It was morning
And everything was forgotten.

Sarah Padday (12)
Hazlegrove Preparatory School, Sparkford

A Fire

The fire touches the walls and heats up the building
It goes up like it is climbing a ladder
It is as hot as the sun (but not as far away)
It eats up the buildings and factories
And looks as if it is eating up its dinner.

Henry Willis (10)
Hazlegrove Preparatory School, Sparkford

The Storm

The wind is coming, clouds are running
The trees are swaying, the grass is whistling
Bang, bang, lightning comes.

Hurricane, hurricane shouts and bangs
Races into the little town
Rips and tears the houses
The houses slowly turn to ashes.

Eventually the sun dances onto the land
And the flowers sing.

Sam Jones (11)
Hazlegrove Preparatory School, Sparkford

Lostprophets

Lostprophets voice is in the air
The singer's voice is everywhere
The fast beat of the rock drummer
A quick slap of the bass guitar's thunder
The electric guitar screaming
The keyboard steaming.

Harry Charlier (11)
Hazlegrove Preparatory School, Sparkford

The Storm

The rain spluttered
The wind howled
The river started sprinting like a rough sea.

Babies screamed
Children chattered
While women ran into their gardens
To get the washing off the line.

Alice Lane (11)
Hazlegrove Preparatory School, Sparkford

The Motorbike

The motorbike sat in the darkness
The lights hammered into the room
The motorbike crawled out onto the drive
The bike roared into life
It chewed up the gravel
It sprinted past the hedges
The motorbike ignored the hitchhikers
The sun sang in the sky
The flowers frolicked by the road
The bike crunched the shale back to the garage
The lights disappeared as quickly as they had appeared.

Alex Wicking (10)
Hazlegrove Preparatory School, Sparkford

The Clock

I ticked
The minute-hand crawled around my face
As half-term ended, the whole class stared at me
Chanting
As the second hands closed in on 4pm
10, 9, 8, 7, 6, 5, 4, 3, 2, 1, zero!

Christopher Black (10)
Hazlegrove Preparatory School, Sparkford

Hyena

High cackle
Blades of steel
Short fur
Has no purr
Quick racer
Antelope masher
It has no test
To be the best.

Hugh Barran (11)
Hazlegrove Preparatory School, Sparkford

Chocolate

The chocolate looked longingly at the children
As if saying, *eat me, eat me*
Sitting there on the table
Hoping that someone would come along and eat it.

Looking sweetly at everyone
There, alone on the table
There is an explanation for this -
It was only a crumb.

Flora Cohen (10)
Hazlegrove Preparatory School, Sparkford

The Factory

The factory was hungry from all the movement inside it
When it was fed it jumped for joy
At night it slept like a log.
In the morning its insides rumbled
In the winter its sides shivered
When it rained it got soaked
At night on New Year's Day
It partied until morning.

Ellen-Jane Robinson (11)
Hazlegrove Preparatory School, Sparkford

The Storm

The storm covered the sky in black
As it roared through the wood
And chewed up the trees
When the sun came out
It shone over the land
The kids came out to play
There were picnics and kites flying.

Edmund Lawson (10)
Hazlegrove Preparatory School, Sparkford

Summertime

Sunny skies
Temperature highs
Cool shades
People bathe
Suntan lotion
Lazy motion
Barbecued food
Changes mood
Shirt and shorts
Always worn
Summertime
Is what I like.

Adam Soanes (11)
Hazlegrove Preparatory School, Sparkford

Fox

A chicken masher
A fence smasher
A rabbit lasher
A night snatcher.

Freddie Ward (10)
Hazlegrove Preparatory School, Sparkford

Cheetah And Cubs

Quickly creeps a cheetah secretly towards the zebra
Then at that particular moment the cheetah pounces, attacking its prey
The cheetah eats the zebra
Quickly feeding it to his cubs
Then searches for food again.

Ellie Daymond (10)
Hillcrest Primary School, Totterdown

Why Is School So Boring?

Why is school so boring?
Is it maths? Is it literacy?
I'm nearly snoring
Why is school so boring?
I'm told to do my work
But some people make me smirk!
'Stay and do your work,' they say
Why can't I have it my way?
Why is school so boring?

Charlie Green (9)
Hillcrest Primary School, Totterdown

Orange

Orange is tropical
Just like the jungle
Bouncy and lively
I don't know why
Maybe a rainbow floating in the sky
All types of butterfly
Lizards and fish everywhere
Orange is tropical
Just like the jungle
You can't resist it.

Molly Highmore (10)
Hillcrest Primary School, Totterdown

Happiness

Happiness is yellow
It tastes of apple pie and sweets
And smells of creamy vanilla soda
Happiness looks like a sunny day on the beach
Happiness feels like joy.

Hapi Murphy (9)
Hillcrest Primary School, Totterdown

The Slinker

The slinker is neither man nor beast
His eyes are pools of silver darkness
He steals away like the shadow of death in-between
                              tumble-down houses
His prey is nought but the vague shapes of others of both living
                              and dead
He moves in a cloak of darkness made of the velvet night sky
No face has he, no soul, no life
Just empty darkness.

Daisy Wilson McNeal (10)
Hillcrest Primary School, Totterdown

Sweet Little Gerbil

Sweet little gerbil
Not making a sound
Sniffing the air
Running happily around.

Soft and fluffy
Multicoloured too
Sweet little gerbil
I love you.

Ettie Webb (9)
Hillcrest Primary School, Totterdown

Arsenal

In the football ground Arsenal beat Man U
For Arsenal that's easy to do
Then Chelsea came along all dressed in blue
Then Arsenal thrashed them 4-2
Arsenal will never lose
They are unbeatable.

Aidan Harrison (9)
Hillcrest Primary School, Totterdown

Young Writers - Little Laureates Verses From South West England

Happiness

Happiness is like dancing on the sun
It tastes like ice cream sundae freshly made
It smells like flowers on the fresh grass
Happiness looks like the sun gleaming brightly
Happiness sounds like the happy music blaring at the beach
Happiness is like everyone having a great time.

Ellen Hulme (9)
Hillcrest Primary School, Totterdown

The Daleks

D aleks are forever
A man called Davros made them
L ike making lolly
E xterminate, exterminate, they say when they . . .
K ill their enemies, their creature inside is a . . .
S lithery mutant - they're not just metal.

David Jeffery-Hughes (10)
Hillcrest Primary School, Totterdown

What Am I?

All soft like a duvet
Cosy like a bed
Fluffy like a bunny
But I live above your head.

Planes soar past me
Rockets pass through me
I make the water
That's handy to use
I make rivers higher
And puddles in your shoes . . .
What am I?

Holly Selswyn-Chater (9)
Hillcrest Primary School, Totterdown

Shining Red

The glistening red shine in the pitch-black darkness
The fascinating perfect shine of one of the most famous Italian
icons ever

To be made as a person machine
It is . . . a Ferrari.

Auzair Arshad (9)
Hillcrest Primary School, Totterdown

Red

Red is anger, love and heat
It scalds when it comes into your touch
But soothes when it meets your gaze
Red is the taste of fiery peppers
But is heard as a soft heartbeat
Red is a rose and the Devil that roams my life.

Eleanor Bailey (9)
Hillcrest Primary School, Totterdown

Green

Green, the colour of laziness
Jungles, palm trees, the sea
Lying on the sandy ground
Gazing up into space
You on your own
Your heart beats slowly
Peace and quiet
All alone.

Siân David (10)
Hillcrest Primary School, Totterdown

Game - Haiku

Hey, you want to play?
Yeah, Hooray I want to play
All right, let's play mate.

Lukasz Filipiak (10)
Hillcrest Primary School, Totterdown

A Valentine's Day Poem

V alentine's Day is a day for love and kindness
A ll around us couples walk
L oving one another - bliss
E very day is very special
N o arguments I hope
T ime is of the essence to get all the presents
I ntimate cosy chats with your loved ones
N o more shops have presents and cards for sale
E xtra special gifts for you and me
S ending roses for your loved one

D ozens of cards with no names on them
A lways trying to find who sent them
Y ap, yap goes the dog as my Valentine cards get posted
    through the door.

Senara Montgomery (10)
Kea Community Primary School, Truro

My Winter Poem

W inter is so dull and grey
I t's cold and windy every day
N ights are bitter, short and wet
T hough it should snow, the news has bet.
E ven though it sounds so bad
R eally it's a nice season, the feeling makes me glad.

Erika Jillian Mangat (9)
Kea Community Primary School, Truro

Haunted House

I went through the garden gate
I turned around but it was too late
The gate had slammed shut
My arms and knees were cut
As I tripped on the garden stones
I heard terrible groans
I got to the door a hand I saw
Before entering the mansion of *doom!*

Inside a chill went through my bones
I heard someone screaming in high-pitched tones
I walked towards the sound
And a girl I found
But what scared me the most
Was that she was a ghost
A vampire flew through the door
And glided across the polished floor
And said, 'My darling, I'll love you for all my life
If you come away now and be my wife?'
I was shocked beyond belief
A vampire and a ghost, *good grief!*

Rianne Shelley (11)
Kea Community Primary School, Truro

I'd Like To Be A Car

I'd like to be a racing car
To travel fast and never be last
I'd be bright red with a massive V8
So I'd never be late
I'd have alloy wheels and leather trim
And take all my friends out for a spin
If I was a Ford I'd be very bored
Better a Porsche and drive with force.

Tom Daniel (10)
Kea Community Primary School, Truro

Our Teacher Is Like No Other Teacher

Our teacher's like no other teacher we have seen
She likes to wear costumes from last Hallowe'en
While shouting a word, she'll dance with a broom
Then sprinkle confetti all over the room.

Our teacher is either completely insane
Or some kind of genius with oodles of brain
But whether it's madness or magical powers
We don't think it matters, we're glad that she's ours.

Morwenna Albury (11)
Kea Community Primary School, Truro

It's In The Cupboard

It's in the cupboard
I bet it'll be smothered
In slime that is grey
And a beard just like hay.

It's gonna come out
With a face like a trout
Teeth the size of swords
And hair as thick as cords.

My eyes were covered
I crept to the cupboard
I was going to get a scare
Suddenly I saw a . . .
Teddy bear!

Rory McLean (11)
Kea Community Primary School, Truro

The Calm Oceans

Bubbly sea calmly washing up onto the dry, sandy shoreline
Where crabs play happily
Darting, multicoloured fish shimmer in the golden light
As they swim through the delicate coral.
Dolphins gracefully diving in and out of the swirling sea
Like a piece of toast flying out of the toaster
Joyfully jellyfish glide to the deep blue
Using their long stinging legs as flippers
Swishing water in beautiful shades of sapphire and emerald
Against the damp sand
Whales slowly use their fins to float through the misty aqua
In the cloudy rock pools, starfish heavily suck up to the dull grey rocks
Murky seaweed tangling up in lobsters' stiff arms
The entire peaceful beach is mute.

Bethany Addey (11)
Kea Community Primary School, Truro

The Peregrine

So slow in your normal flight
But with a flick of your tempering tail
You will dive so fast and will never fail.
So bend those pointed, broad-based wings
And chase your prey until it falls.
Hold it, then eat it with your dreadful tools
The talons you use to grip and your beak to tear.
Then fly to your small, loving, fluffy chicks
Go on, after all, you are the cheetah of the air!

Oscar Marsh (10)
Kea Community Primary School, Truro

Stadium Of Dreams

At the Stadium of Dreams I bounce so high
I feel I can touch the stars
Forward flips, somersaults, handstands -
I feel like an Olympic gymnast.

At the Stadium of Dreams I take a try
Feeling like a world-class player
I line up my kick like Jonny -
Up, up and over the bar.

At the Stadium of Dreams I slide the toboggan run
Wearing my country's colour
Icy cold water carrying me
To the end of the track.

At the Stadium of Dreams penalty shoot-outs
Goals galore
Weaving and dodging through the players . . .
Stadium of Dreams - my garden - 1,001 games to be played.

Nick Spencer (10)
Kea Community Primary School, Truro

Seasons

The trees sprout leaves that are gold and brown
They fly through the old church town
Now the sea is frozen over
The grass is cold as ice
The winter breeze blows over all
That catches in its sights.
Snowdrops glisten from all around
It shows that Jack Frost has been in town.
Thank goodness it is summer
The warmth is back in town
It's time at last to start to clown.

Scarlette Reed (10)
Kea Community Primary School, Truro

Australian Football League

A ustralian Football League is the most awesome sport
F ootball is similar to this
L ions are my favourite team

R uck-rover is my position I have to follow the ball, attacking
and defending

U mpires are the equivalent of referees
L uckily Lions won three years in a row
E ngland has no idea how good this sport is
S upersonic sport of the world - AFL!

Benji Neal (11)
Kea Community Primary School, Truro

Cats' Travels

One day our cats packed their bags
Hired a Jag and took a ferry to France
They ate snails and frogs' legs
And drank too much wine
And rested under the shade of a pine.
They caught a plane to Africa
And set off on safari
And lived with a family of meerkats
In the desert of the Kalahari.
In New York, they lived the high life
And shopped until they dropped
Then took a jumbo back home to us
And fell asleep by the fire
And got a lot of fuss.

Henry George (11)
Kea Community Primary School, Truro

Stormy Seas

Frothing seas smashing against the cliffs
Tossing terrified ships, threatening to capsize
Down in the deep and darkened ocean
Fish are trembling with fear
Still the foaming waves pound against the rocks
As if an earthquake is shaking under the navy waters
Huge waves crash down on the shore
Sweeping back the stony sand
Rain pours down onto the violent surface of the sea
And wind howls like a wolf
Lightning flashes, illuminating the scene for a second
Thunder crashes, like enormous cymbals
But soon the sea seems to tire itself out
It slows down its energetic movement
Clouds begin to drift away to reveal the sun
The storm on the coast is finally over
But plenty of driftwood is washed up on the beach
Remains of the vicious storm.

Alison Johnston (10)
Kea Community Primary School, Truro

Watch Out!

The eagle soaring through the sky,
Swooping down through the clouds,
High up there gliding around,
Seeks his prey and squawks a deafening sound.
He nose-dives through the air,
Catches his prey with his claws
And squeezes until it is no more.

Arthur Lawry (10)
Kea Community Primary School, Truro

Summer

Emerald glinting sea, golden sandy beach
It would be perfect if there were palm trees waving just out of reach
Smell of cooking sausages, hot sand burning our feet
The dog, me, my sister and brother, Mum and Dad all feel the heat
The hum of bugs, the buzz of bees
All of the squirrels scamper all around the tall beautiful trees
Dazzling acrobatic dragonflies, brightly coloured butterflies
Some of the cats try to stalk them but they will have to jump very high
Multicoloured flowers, lush green grass
All of the horses in the fields roll and frolic in the soft green grass
Hundreds of pigeons, crows fly in pairs
The seagulls are here, the pests are back, their cries of joy fill the air!

Phoebe Maggs (10)
Kea Community Primary School, Truro

The Scariest Night

In the silent narrow street
I am sweating from the heat
I can see a flashing light
It is clear because it's night.

I can hear a sorry moan
Now I know I'm not alone
I don't dare look around
Because I'm frightened of the sound.

My heart is thumping like a drum
I want to break into a run
I stop dead in my tracks
I am determined to turn back.

I turn around to see
Others just as scared as me
All the ghouls that I have seen
Are dressed up for Hallowe'en.

Hannah Susnjara (10)
Kea Community Primary School, Truro

The Treacherous Sea

The treacherous sea swallows boats whole
Yachts thundering down to the seabed smashing into pieces
Tugboats are struggling in a current trying to pull them into a whirlpool
The waves toss higher and higher, pulling things into
their mighty grasp
The Titanic is crashing in to an iceberg, splitting into three
Birds are swept into the sea then turned into skeletons
Submarines on the ocean floor now curled up with an octopus
The sea tossing back and forth, making men seasick
A killer shark leaps on a boat eating the sailor whole
Then the boat is tugged into the current, the cabin, the sail, all
The salty air, the salty sea, the tide, the water, the foam
I'm feeling rather ill now
It's such a stormy night on this treacherous sea.

Henry Eades (9)
Kea Community Primary School, Truro

Creatures

I love all kinds of creatures
Monkeys, pigs, cats and dogs
They all have different features
My friend likes dogs and frogs.

Monkeys can swing high
Right up to the clouds
And touch the sky
Monkeys can be loud.

Pigs can be quite dirty
Rolling in the mud
If I had a pig, I would call it Gertie
They need some soap suds.

Cats and dogs don't get on
They scratch and hiss and bite
Especially my dog Ron
Him and the cat always fight.

Jade Whalley (10)
Kea Community Primary School, Truro

Surfing Survival

The waves broke heavily above my head
I panicked to rise to the surface, to smell and breathe the fresh salty air
I couldn't see, for the light was fading in front of me
Then came another huge 15ft wave, tossing and turning me
                                                with enormous power
The waves just wouldn't stop coming at me
I saw a surfboard floating in the terrible waters
Someone had become a victim of the sea
I swam with all my might to the surfboard, I hauled myself on
I held on tight while the wave took the surfboard to shore.

Eddie Coombs (10)
Kea Community Primary School, Truro

Traction Engine

A giant monster appeared out of the deep fog
Steam pouring from its big black funnel
The smell of burning wood fills the air
Twenty children could not beat it at tug-of-war.

Joe D'Souza (10)
Kea Community Primary School, Truro

Computer Kid

C ame home from school and *flash* . . . I disappeared
O n the computer again
M um complained, 'Josh, come and do your homework
P lease come,' Mum yelled
U nfortunately I didn't hear her
T oo busy playing on the computer
E veryone my age understands
R un home, switch the computer on and play, play, play.

Josh Neal (10)
Kea Community Primary School, Truro

My Blissful Holiday!

The soft blue sea washes with white waves
At the end of the beach there are undiscovered caves
The soft white sand swishes around the rocks
The freezing water fills my socks
As sea creatures crawl across the beach
I climb to the top of the rocks, far as I can reach
I splash in the waves and make myself wet
I stay at the beach, it's now sunset
The sparkling sea makes my eyes shine
The beach feels so blissful, the beach feels like mine
The moon shines down glistening light
The little children take down their kite
Though quite late, people are still here
Then the tide comes in ever so near
The cliffs are so tall they tower over me
The cliffs are as tall as I can see
We walk across the seaside
The little crabs crawl and hide
The soft sand between my toes
The harsh winds blow against my nose
We pack up our things and head into the night
We look at the beach, what a beautiful sight!

Lucy Topham (9)
Kea Community Primary School, Truro

The Monster

Sharp spiky claws
Lives in murky moors
Dirty scruffy hairs
It bites, it rips, it tears
Sharp bloody fangs
It chomps, crunches, bangs
Mouldy smelly feet
He's a monster
You wouldn't like to meet!

Quincy Smith (9)
Kea Community Primary School, Truro

Friends

F riends are people you can trust
R ight from the start, everyone needs a friend
I n their heart
E ndless friendship will help you not be apart
N ever make your best friend cry
D on't let your friendship die
S tand with your friend

F orever until the end
O ther people will want to be your friend so just
R emember friends are special and
E veryone would like a friend, so be
V ery nice to your best friend because they will be
E xtremely nice to you too and
R emember, they are your friend and you can trust them.

Catherine Marston (9)
Kea Community Primary School, Truro

My Bunny Is Called Ralphy

Ralphy is my bunny
He is so very funny
He sometimes licks my face
And he runs around the place
He likes to live inside
And likes to play and hide
He sits in his hutch
But doesn't do much
And that is the story
Of my bunny called Ralphy.

Sam Adams (9)
Kea Community Primary School, Truro

Chocolate

The creamy chocolate, so delicious and sweet
I try to be good so I can have it as a treat
There is dark chocolate, white chocolate and milk chocolate
I like milk chocolate the best
But I will still eat the rest.

Jordan Gaslonde (10)
Kea Community Primary School, Truro

There Once Was A . . .

There once was a snail
That was very slow
He left a slimy trail
Wherever he would go!

There once was a cat
That had soft fur
He wore a Mexican hat
And had the loudest ever purr!

There once was a dog
A coat of brown and tan
That always jumped like a frog
That was chewing a cola can!

I like my silly animals
They always make me snigger
But my favourite of them all
Is my best mate Tigger!

Beth Richards (8)
Kea Community Primary School, Truro

My Best Friend

I have a best friend
We play every day
Chase the ball and catch.

I tell him all my secrets
He cuddles me when I'm sad
We watch DVDs together
He sits with me when I play PlayStation.

I feed him when he's hungry
And snuggle him by the fire
He waits for me to let him in -
Saying, 'Please' and 'Thank you' as he goes past.

My best friend is Bruiser
My best friend is my cat.

James Spencer (7)
Kea Community Primary School, Truro

A Winter's Day

Crashing seas, huge waves
Thundering onto the shore
Wind howling through the trees
Sand blowing across the beach
Surfers carving their way into shore
Fishermen tucked safely in the harbour.

William House (10)
Kea Community Primary School, Truro

A Dragon

The fire from the dragon is like a red-hot furnace
The smooth scaly skin all blue and worn
Claws like metal spikes sharper than knives.

Christopher Marshall (11)
Kea Community Primary School, Truro

My Teddy Bear Mr B

I have a favourite teddy, his name is Mr B
When I travel far, he goes along with me
I really, really love him, whatever people say
I don't really care cos he always makes my day
He has a cousin Cuthbert, a super, super bear
When they're together, they're a really naughty pair!

Mr B, Mr B, Mr B and me
Mr B, Mr B, Mr B and me!

He has a big, big brother whose Christian name is Ted
He sleeps in his own bed with his favourite doggy toy Ned
His favourite TV programme is the Superteds
He watches it on Sunday nights but never goes to bed
He lives in St Piran and goes to school as well
He has a girlfriend Eloise but please don't, please don't tell
He has a best friend James, remember Fluffy too
When they're together they're a super, super crew!

Felicity Freeborn (8)
Kea Community Primary School, Truro

My Gerbil

Jerry my gerbil sleeps in his cage
A fragile little ball of fur
Waking, he scampers out looking for his food
Nibbling and crunching he cracks open a nut
Now he is dashing about in his wheel
Travelling nowhere at all
Scrabbling in the sawdust, he meets the glass at the bottom
Still trying to tunnel through
Tired out, he goes back to his sleep
Dreaming of the next day.

Susannah Johnston (8)
Kea Community Primary School, Truro

My Dream

I heard the wind one night
And galloping hooves too
The horse's breath against me
As if it could understand every word

I heard the wind one night
And trotting hooves too
And I could feel its warm coat
As on and on I flew

I heard the wind one night
And prancing hooves too
And it nuzzled me again and again
And in my dream it was true.

Katie Brown (7)
Kea Community Primary School, Truro

Eloise

Eloise my teddy
She is never ever ready
We are always in a hurry
She really makes me worry.

Her fur is soft and white
And she loves to fly a kite
She really loves her honey
And she's got a pet bunny.

She gives me great big hugs
She really likes her bugs
Her favourite are the bees
But the flowers make her sneeze.

In the sun we have great fun
So come and join us everyone.

Isabel Wellings (7)
Kea Community Primary School, Truro

At The Pirates

Jogging onto the pitch, I hear the crowd cheering and chanting.
Voices shouting a rhythm with no tune,
Cold from the gushing wind and driving rain,
Nervous, butterflies fluttering in my stomach,
I can see the stadium stretching up into the cold sky.
Thousands of people looking down at me.
The pitch is a green sea with fish darting around
Red, blue and yellow, chasing in and out
Sprinting, pushing, tackling and kicking
A tidal wave of cheers when a try is scored.
The shriek of a referee's whistle echoes around,
I leave the pitch, proud and numb,
A toothy grin on my freezing face,
A brilliant victory for my team.

Tom Knuckey (8)
Kea Community Primary School, Truro

Inside My Magic Box

A dragon lived in a great castle
Horn on head, spikes on back
Shining teeth, beady eyes
Scales of gold glistening in the sun
Bones moon-white laid in corridors
Claws as sharp as daggers.

Tom Praed-Mather (8)
Kea Community Primary School, Truro

Horse

H orse galloping in the wind
O h what a beautiful sight
R unning and cantering
S ound of its beating heart
E very child's dream.

Imogen Robson (7)
Kea Community Primary School, Truro

The Magic Box
(Based on 'Magic Box' by Kit Wright)

I will put in the box . . .
The splash of a dolphin in the calmest, bluest ocean
The sudden pop of a party popper at the coolest party ever
The touch of my spotty rabbit's velvety nose
The feel of my cuddly dog's soft fur
The delicious smell of hot chocolate cake straight from the oven.

I will put in the box . . .
The sip of the brownest, fizziest Coke in the world
The gulp of the coolest lemonade on a hot summer's day
The lick of the juiciest, fruitiest ice lolly
The taste of a zesty cheesecake fresh from the freezer.

I will put in the box . . .
Daffodils growing in the winter
A camel in the Arctic
A polar bear in the desert
An elephant in Matalan.

The box is made from beautiful smelling pine wood
With sapphires and rubies in the corners
And a great big star in the middle made with lots of pretty things
I shall take a journey in the box
To a beautiful tropical island
And swim in the crystal-clear sea.

Rachel Addey (9)
Kea Community Primary School, Truro

Holidays

Holidays are great
Holidays are fun
Holidays in the sun
Sitting by the pool
Trying to keep cool
Eating lots of ice cream
Holidays rule!

Phoebe Staines (7)
Kea Community Primary School, Truro

My Pet Is A . . .

My pet is my moon, my stars, everyday life
She lies on my bed with dignity and no aggressiveness
Her hair is soft and silky, but she runs away now and again
She is there when I'm happy, sad or mad
She loves to lick my face and my toes too
She would sit happily on a log
Cos my pet is a . . .
Dog!

Daisy Cochran Scarratt (9)
Kea Community Primary School, Truro

New Day Spell

One great grumpy gorilla
Five cute chubby chinchillas
Mix and mix until green
Then add a bucket full of cream
Then add a bit of spicy spice
As well as ten or more dead baby mice
Once it has gone a deep dark brown
Add the jewels from the king and queen's crown
And if you want a bit of taste
Add a load of wallpaper paste
And if you are daring enough to risk it
Drop in some crumbs of a digestive biscuit
Then mix and mix, then drink it all down
And tomorrow you will end up sleeping in town.

Davinia Davey (9)
Kea Community Primary School, Truro

Pets

Cute fluffy guinea pigs
Running round the hutch
Cute fluffy guinea pigs
Eating a bit too much.

Soft little hamsters
Running in the ball
Soft little hamsters
Halfway down the hall.

Cute fluffy kittens
Playing with some string
Cute fluffy kittens
Playing out in spring.

Soft little puppies
Are definitely the best
Soft little puppies
Better than the rest!

Anna Gowenlock (8)
Kea Community Primary School, Truro

Dogs

Dogs, they chase the cats
And ignore the rats
They like bouncy balls
And they like jumping over walls
They like to bury their bones
Close to their homes
They are cuddly and cute
And sometimes wear a suit
Did you know
They like snow!

Katie Croft-Hill (8)
Kea Community Primary School, Truro

Pets

Some pets are small
Some pets are tall
Some pets are heavy
Some weigh next to nothing at all!

Some pets are black
Some pets are white
Some are dark brown
Some are light.

Some pets are quite vicious
Some can be quite calm
Some are really kind
Some can't do any harm!

But the ones I like best . . .
Are the ones that are cute
That lick you and nip you
And chew on your boot!

Lily Sullivan (8)
Kea Community Primary School, Truro

Molly

I have a dog called Molly
And she is nearly two
If I play in my garden
I always wear shoes
(She treats the garden as her loo)
You have to be careful not to step in her poo
She's white and fat and plays with my cat
I love my dog called Molly.

Will Drury (10)
Kea Community Primary School, Truro

Kernow

What does Cornwall mean to you?
To me it means . . .
Long sandy beaches with surfers on the turquoise-blue waves
Succulent, warming pasties from W C Rowe
Lovely walks, watching wildlife
Fat seals silently sprawled all over the place at Goodrevy
Amazing squirrels at Tehidy
The brilliant, breathtaking Hornet roller coaster at Flambards
Hedgehogs, ice creams and smiley faces
On a hot day at Chapelporth beach, yummy
The buzzard, a beautiful bird
And the squawking interfering seagulls - how could I forget!
Vicious rugby, not my kind of thing . . .
Come on Cornwall Pirates anyway
The magical Mousehole Christmas lights, truly unforgettable
But the best thing about Cornwall is . . .
Home, friends and family.

Lauren Thompson (10)
Kea Community Primary School, Truro

Haunted House

H aunted houses have . . .
A spooky stone spiral staircase
U nwanted visitors
N ightmares and scary thoughts
T hings that go bump in the night
E normous energy forces
D usty, dank books filled with chants and potions

H orrifying
O dorous
U ndead
S talking for all
E ternity.

Edward Jose (11)
Kea Community Primary School, Truro

Chocolate Cake Charm

Round about the cauldron go
In the Cadbury's chocolate throw
Thick custard with some chocolate snow
Sprinkles with a chocolate glow
Fresh butter with a flow.

Chocolate flake with birthday cake
Covered with dust so great

Make a perfect cake, so bright and light
Go to France to get the wine
Then put the Smarties in the bake
To make the yummy gorgeous cake
Melted chocolate in the middle
While you listen to this riddle

Chocolate flake with birthday cake
Covered with dust so great.

Thomas Roles (10)
St Mary's Primary School, Bridgwater

Fear Vs Courage

Fear is blood-red
It smells like strong fire
It tastes like sour cream
It feels like bullets piercing my heart
It sounds like a war has begun
Fear lives in a deep dark dungeon.

Courage is bright brave yellow
It smells like freshly squeezed lemons
It tastes like melted chocolate
It feels like having a first love
It sounds like classical music
Courage lives in my heart.

Ryan Deans (10)
St Mary's Primary School, Bridgwater

Tiger

(Inspired by 'Cat Began' by Andrew Matthews)

The tiger began
He stole the roar of thunder
He stole the loudness of eight men
He stole the snap of fireworks
For his voice.

He stole the softness of the grass
He stole the orange of the sunset
He stole the stripes of coal
For his coat.

He stole your breathing when you were asleep
He stole the sound of grass in the wind
He stole the sound of panting
For his run.

He stole the burnt wood of a fire
He stole the blackness of a crow
He stole the baldness of a ball
For his eyes.

He stole the sharpness of a sword
He stole the glint of silver
He stole the strength of a bulletproof vest
For his paw.

The tiger was made.

Luke Dyer (10)
St Mary's Primary School, Bridgwater

Rabbit In Creation

(Inspired by 'Cat Began' by Andrew Matthews)

Rabbit started . . .

For his eyes
He took the red of rubies
He took the sparkling of flowing water
And he took the shape of little beads.

For his fur
He took the comfort of a duvet
He took the softness of cotton wool
He took the smoothness of silk.

For his walk
He took the hop of a kangaroo
He took the sprint of a cheetah
He took the strut of a cat.

For his claws
He took the sharpness of a hawk
He took the shininess of a panther
He took the shape of a hook.

Rabbit was made.

Luke Payne (11)
St Mary's Primary School, Bridgwater

The Elephant
(Inspired by 'Cat Began' by Andrew Matthews)

She took the wrinkles from the old man's face
She took the colour from the dark grey sky
And built her skin.

She took the banging from the hammer
To echo the stamping of her feet
She took the thick tree trunks
And make her strong sturdy legs.

She took the glittering of the stars
And the blackness of the berries
And painted her eyes.

She took the sheets from the washing line
Flapping in the breeze
And made her ears.

She took a stretchy clay spout
From the teapot
And made her big long trunk.

Courtney Boobyer (10)
St Mary's Primary School, Bridgwater

Love And Hate

Love is metallic pink
It smells like a red rose
It tastes like Belgian chocolates
It sounds like classical music
It feels like a cruise around the world
Love lives on every Valentine's Day.

Hate is red lava
It smells like an explosion of gas
It tastes like very strong poison
It sounds like guns firing
It feels like a tidal wave
Hate lives in the bottom of the Arctic Ocean.

Austin Hodges (11)
St Mary's Primary School, Bridgwater

Monkey In The Making

(Inspired by 'Cat Began' by Andrew Matthews)

He took the softness of the pillows
And the roughness of sandpaper
His coat was made.

He took the glimmering of the stars
He took the sharpness of a needle
And the water of the rain
His face was made.

He took the screeching of the children
And the howling of the wind
His voice was made.

He took the wrinkles of a tree
And the size of sausages
His hands were made.

Monkey was born.

Jacob Sidebotham (10)
St Mary's Primary School, Bridgwater

Anger And Happiness

Anger is dark red
It smells like burning black smoke
It tastes like mouldy, rotten cheese
It sounds like a volcano erupting
It feels like needles piercing your head
Anger lives in a dark, bottomless pit.

Happiness is pale blue
It smells like exotic fruits
It tastes like real Belgian chocolate
It sounds like music from a faraway land
It feels like a warm smoothing bubblebath
It lives in the centre of your heart.

Jake Gardener (10)
St Mary's Primary School, Bridgwater

My Magic Box

(Based by 'Magic Box' by Kit Wright)

In my box I will keep . . .
The colours of a rainbow
The questions you ask your grandparents
The touch of a newborn kitten.

In my box I will keep . . .
The silk of a wedding dress
The sip of my favourite drink
The feathers from a phoenix.

In my box I will keep . . .
The love from Valentine's Day
The light of a lovely summer sun
The shout of a happy child.

Finally, in my box I will keep . . .
The smile of a best friend.

Courtney Barrow (10)
St Mary's Primary School, Bridgwater

My Magic Box

(Based on 'Magic Box' by Kit Wright)

I will place in my box . . .
A proud camel walking over the scorching desert
The swish of the deep dark ocean
And the magical colours of a rainbow.

I will place in my box . . .
A galloping black horse
The brightest twinkling star
And a leaping dolphin.

I will place in my box . . .
A tall palm tree swishing in the breeze
The beautiful angel shimmering
And a silken cloud floating in the clear blue sky.

Jessica Dunn (10)
St Mary's Primary School, Bridgwater

War And Peace

War is as grey as a cloudy sky
It smells like burnt coal
It tastes like fresh blood
It sounds like the shot of a gun
It feels like falling into a red-hot volcano
War lives in a barrel of gunpowder.

Peace is duck-egg blue
It smells like freshly cut grass
It tastes like melted chocolate
It sounds like birds singing in the morning
It feels like cold weather
Peace lives in a hippie's camper van.

Charlie Fletcher (10)
St Mary's Primary School, Bridgwater

War And Peace

War is blood-red
It smells like burning corpses
It tastes like rotting flesh
It sounds like screams and gunshots
It feels like a permanent nightmare
It lives in the deepest inferno.

Peace is shining gold
It smells like your favourite meal
It tastes like a McDonald's banquet
It sounds like laughter
It feels like a never-ending dream
It lives in the brightest happiness.

Wesley Williams (11)
St Mary's Primary School, Bridgwater

In My Magic Box

(Based on 'Magic Box' by Kit Wright)

In my magic box I will put . . .
The colours of the rainbow
Love from a first kiss
A hot summer's day
And happiness from your heart.

In my box I will keep . . .
My first pair of shoes
My earliest smile wrapped in silk
A family portrait from long ago
With my mum and dad.

I will treasure in my box . . .
The courage of a magical unicorn
The sound of children laughing
A spider's web full of sparkling diamonds
And a shooting star to wish upon.

My box shall be made out of . . .
The whitest fluffiest cloud
The points of the sharpest pins
A multicoloured fish from the Mississippi
And in every corner there will be a secret.

Zoe Rowe (10)
St Mary's Primary School, Bridgwater

Pick On Me, Why?

There's a bully in the playground
He comes up straight to me,
I say, 'Hello,' and what does he say?
'Do you want to be bullied?'

I run away and try to hide
And stay away from him
He finds me somewhere
And punches me in the face,
Then he starts to grin!

Luke Shaw (10)
St Mary's Primary School, Bridgwater

The Magic Box

(Based on 'Magic Box' by Kit Wright)

In my box I will keep . . .
A glittering star from the darkest sky
The feel of a green velvet curtain
And the shimmer of purple fairy dust.

In my box I will keep . . .
Good friends' voices
The sound of applause
And a gentle cloud over a mountain top.

In my box I will keep . . .
My sister's laugh
The feel of my cat's fur
And the necklace from my eleventh birthday.

In my box I will keep . . .
A speckled bird's egg
A head-dress woven from summer grass
And the pot of gold from the end of the rainbow.

Sarah Mansell (11)
St Mary's Primary School, Bridgwater

Why Always Me?

Why always me?
Is it because I have fuzzy hair?
Is it because I'm short?
Is it because you are frustrated?
Is it that you're bored?

Why always me?
Is it because I wear goofy glasses?
Is it because I am white?
Is it because my hair is ginger?
Is it because I am different?

Why always me?

Amy Scriven (10)
St Mary's Primary School, Bridgwater

Victim

Why me?
I hate bullies
I wish I never lived here
What do I look like?
Why don't they pick on someone else?

Why me?
I bet they couldn't pick on me alone
Should I leave my house?
I'm too scared to tell my mum
Being bullied isn't cool.

Why me?
I am too afraid to tell my teacher
Being alive should never have happened
What if they find out where I live?
I want to be buried alive!
Why me?
Why me?

Jayden Parr (10)
St Mary's Primary School, Bridgwater

What's Wrong With Me?

What's wrong with me?
Do I smell?
Do they think I make a magic spell?
Do they need some help?
Do they think I tell on them?

What's wrong with me?
Do I have bad breath?
Am I deaf?
Do they think I am shy?
Do they think I tell a lie?

What's wrong with me?
Do they think I'm weak?
Do they think I'm a freak?
Am I in a stress?
Would they think I learn less?

What's wrong with me?

Fern Thompson (11)
St Mary's Primary School, Bridgwater

Why Is It Me?

Why is it me?
I hate bullies
Why am I weak?
Why me?

I like school
But everyone calls me names
I'm always kicked
My legs are black and blue
Why me?

Pick on someone else
Leave me alone!
I bet you're a coward
Lonely too!
Why can't we be friends?
Why me?

Tom Rich (10)
St Mary's Primary School, Bridgwater

Why Me?

Why do you pick on me?
I am not different to anyone else!
Why do you pick on me?
Pick on someone else!

Why is it me?
I wish I wasn't born!
Why is it me?
But I wish I wasn't here.

Why am I different?
I haven't got glasses!
Why am I different?
I am not orange-haired!

What is wrong with me?
Is it because I am dark-skinned?
What is wrong with me?
I really do not know.

Emily Frost (11)
St Mary's Primary School, Bridgwater

The Big Bad Bully

Why does he pick on me?
Is it because I wear my grandad's glasses?
Is it because I have bright, bushy, red hair?
Is it because I like stinky sprouts?
Is it because I'm the size of a six-year-old?
Is it because I support the worst team in the universe?

Why does he pick on me?
Is it because I'm dark-skinned?
Is it because my mum's blind?
Is it because my dad comes from Africa?
Is it because I am a computer nerd and a freak?
Is it because I'm top of the class?

I wish I was never born!
Then the world would be a better place.

Jack Tottle (11)
St Mary's Primary School, Bridgwater

The Bully Poem!

I get bullied but I don't know why
Whenever the bully gets told off
He always tells a lie!

Is it my shoes or is it my top?
Whatever it is
I want it to stop.

Can't he pick on someone else?
Leave people alone
Just stay by himself.

He thinks he's the best
Much better than the rest
He even picks on birds in their nests.

Why does he pick on me?
Can't he see
What a good friend I could really be?

Sophie Jordan (11)
St Mary's Primary School, Bridgwater

I'm The Victim

I'm the victim being picked on
The amount of times I've been hit
My shoulder was shattered, beaten by a wrought iron blade
It was that bully, I was nearly in my grave
Sticks and stones come at my head
I want to be alone (I'd rather be dead)
I'm in the corner; they come at me
Shout, kick and also tease me
I just want to hide for a very long time
And never have to be the victim of this terrible crime.

James Lloyd (10)
St Mary's Primary School, Bridgwater

Why Is It Me?

Why is it me? Why is it me?
Why can't it be he or she?
I am scared
And they are so weird
I always get beaten, see!

I always get a battering
Then they start threatening
Why is it me?
Can't it be he or she?

Why is it me? Why is it me?
Why can't it be he or she?

Pick on that boy over there
I really know you care
Let's be friends, please I want to
Yes you, yes you, yes you.

Why is it me? Why is it me?
Why can't it be he or she?

Bradley Warren (10)
St Mary's Primary School, Bridgwater

She Won't Listen

She pushes me around
She says things, swears even
I tell her, 'I don't like it,' but she won't listen.

She tells me to do her homework and then gets praised for it
She makes me do things I don't want to do
She boasts about herself in front of everyone
She says horrible things to embarrass me
I tell her, 'No, stop that,' but she won't listen.

She says, 'Go and make yourself trip over until I say stop.'
She says, 'Give me your lunch.'
She says, 'Go get me this, go get that.'
I say, 'I don't want to,' but she won't listen.

She tells everyone my secrets
She says I'm ugly
She says a lot of things
I tell her not to, but she won't listen.

Sophie Manship (11)
St Mary's Primary School, Bridgwater

Why Me?

Why me, what did I ever do to him?
I never did anything wrong, did I?
It's bizarre and confuses me.

Why me? I've done all my homework
Been a good little so and so
Why does he always follow me?

Oh why? Oh why? Oh why?
But he's got to feel alone inside,
I expect he needs a friend.

Why don't I go and cheer him up,
On second thought, maybe not,
He'll only say, 'Skedaddle snot.'

Edward Page-Symonds (11)
St Mary's Primary School, Bridgwater

A Delicious Chocolate Cake

Round about the cauldron go
Everybody needs to know
Boil thou first in the charmed pot
Until the water is nice and hot.

How to make a special cake
And just how long it needs to bake.

Add in the flour, sugar, eggs and butter
Stir it in hard until it becomes a batter
Add the chocolate buttons and chips
Pour it into a tin and into the oven
Be careful, do not slip!

How to make a special cake
And just how long it needs to bake.

In the cauldron boil and bubble
No licking the spoon or you're in trouble
Make the icing nice and white
Pipe it on ready for tonight
For a charm of powerful trouble
Like a hell-broth boil and bubble.

How to make a special cake
And just how long it needs to bake.

Laura Hallett (10)
St Mary's Primary School, Bridgwater

My Bully And Me

She always pushes me around,
She stole my only friend,
She took my dinner money,
Will this bullying ever end?

She's broken my best locket,
It was a birthday gift from Mum,
She says I am a loser,
Because I don't chew gum.

She's forever angry with me,
I really don't know why,
I am not the only one
Who feels extremely shy.

She calls me, 'Sally no friends,'
Cos my friend doesn't talk to me,
The biggest question I have to ask
Is, 'What is wrong with me?'

Olivia Tucker (10)
St Mary's Primary School, Bridgwater

Snow

S lowly snow falls
N obody cannot like snow
O n my hand it lands
W onderful crystal-white snow
F lutters like a butterfly
L ower and lower till it reaches the ground
A s soft as a furry fox, the
K ey to winter wonderland
E veryone loves *snow!*

Jess Walter (9)
St Philip's CE Primary School, Bath

The Magic Box

(Based on 'Magic Box' by Kit Wright)

I will put in the box . . .
The first drop of the beautiful golden rain
The ripest red apple
And a baby's first laugh.

I will put in the box . . .
A big blue bunch of bananas
The sight of true love's first kiss
And a springy bounce from a trampoline.

I will put in the box . . .
A violet rose
A strand of a unicorn's fur
And a blue jewellery box that floats.

I will put in the box . . .
The Queen's diamond from her crown
The words from a chapter of a book
And the first flower of spring.

My box is fashioned . . .
From gold, silver and bronze
With sparkles on the lid
And surprises in the corners
Its hinges are the scales of a rainbow fish.

I will fly in my box . . .
To a magical place
Soaring through the fluffy clouds
And when I get there
I will put new things in my box
That I find in the magical place.

Maisie Skuse (10)
St Philip's CE Primary School, Bath

Window Sight

The eerie mist simmers with light
Unaware of the beautiful sight
The moon is low among the stars
You can see the planets, even Mars
The fern trees sway with the breeze
The icy night which makes you freeze
The soil is thrown in the air
While animals scatter, including hares
The fox's beady eyes can only help to stare
The mysterious clouds hover in the sky
Where constellations stay to humans' eyes
The flower petals whizz around
Soon enough to land on the ground
That's what I see from my window.

Jessica Blackwell (9)
St Philip's CE Primary School, Bath

My Happy Family

Mum is teaching Tom to crawl
Dad's in the study waiting for a work call
Alex is a good boy in his room
Em will go and see him soon
Tom is screaming in Mum's face
Dad is tying his shoelace
Alex is thinking he is great
Em is still waiting for her mate
Tom is groaning
Dad is moaning
In the end it's time for tea
Mum is laughing with glee!

Georgia Symonds (9)
St Philip's CE Primary School, Bath

The Magic Box

(Based on 'Magic Box' by Kit Wright)

I will put in the box . . .
The power of the gods
The golden horns of the Minotaur
And a magic silver bird.

I will put in the box . . .
The red skin of a black rhino
The eyeball of a troll
And three golden wishes.

My box is fashioned from . . .
Fire and gold and ice
With jewellery on the lid and sequins
Its hinges are dinosaur bones
I will travel under the sea to Atlantis
Fly over the moon and disappear
To a magical land.

Cameron Davies (9)
St Philip's CE Primary School, Bath

Snow

S ledges for fun
N umb fingers
O n the ground
W inter, winter, winter
F luttering snow
A ngels in the snow
L ush and
L ovely snow.

Olivia Simms (9)
St Philip's CE Primary School, Bath

Snow

S now falling to the ground
N obody cannot like snow
O utside children play
W onderful things happen today
F alling like fairies
L ovely soft snow
A lmost everywhere I go
K ind snow falling down
E verybody must like snow

S oft snow is falling
N o snowmen yet but
O utside children play
W onderful snow is falling down
F luttering down, snow falls
A ngels dance in the sky
L ovely ice on the floor
L ucky snow on the door.

Alyx Ball   (9)
St Philip's CE Primary School, Bath

Snow, Snow

S now, snow
N o one hates snow
O verflow, please, please
W hite and
F luffy
L ovely snow, snow
A nyone loves snow, I wish it would
K eep falling for
E ver and ever.

Nadia Bancroft
St Philip's CE Primary School, Bath

Snow

S now on the ground all crystal-white
N obody can stop me playing in it
O h my, it's cold
W onderful snow
F alling like leaves on the ground
L ying down so cold and damp
A s soft as my furry white rabbit
K eeps falling
E verywhere, wonderful snow!

S ilvery snow
N o one cannot like snow
O nly falls once or twice a year
W onderful white snow
F alling all
A round me
L ike a butterfly
L ovely snow!

Olivia Parkyn (8)
St Philip's CE Primary School, Bath

Snow

S now falling like an angel
N obody could not like it
O h how I love snow
W inter will never end
F loating like a bird
L ovely snow, how I love you
A nyone would like to play in it
K ing of the sky
E xciting snow, how we love you.

Victoria Horroll (9)
St Philip's CE Primary School, Bath

Snowflake

S parkling snow like white sand
N ow it's melting it makes me sad
O n my own in the snow then it turns into
W ater, there's no snow left
F lakes falling like stars
L anding in my hand
A nyone can play with snow
K eys to the North Pole
E veryone likes snow.

Yazmin Moss (8)
St Philip's CE Primary School, Bath

Snowflake Poem

S now falling like a feather
N o one will stop me from playing
O h, it is wonderful, so crispy
W inter wonderland, so crispy
F lakes flutter like a butterfly to the ground
L ike a beautiful white land
A nd everywhere, a
K ey to a winter wonderland
E veryone loves snow.

Sophie Clark (8)
St Philip's CE Primary School, Bath

Snowman

S now is really cold
N ow I'm freezing
O n the way to get a snowball I get hit myself
W ait for someone to pass by, then chuck
M ind you don't get hit
A ll the snow is nearly gone
N o more snowball fights.

Hannah Hewett (7)
St Philip's CE Primary School, Bath

A Snow Poem

S ilvery snow
N obody doesn't like the snow
O utside the snow falls
W inter wonderland
F lutters down
L ike a feather
A nyone allowed to play in the snow
K ey to winter wonderland
E xciting snow, such fun.

Cobi Short (8)
St Philip's CE Primary School, Bath

Snowflake

S ilently snow falls
N obody can hate snow
O n my face it lies
W inter is a wonderful season
F luttering down
L ightly it falls
A s soft as a cushion, a
K ey to winter wonderland
E veryone enjoys *snow!*

Tyra Smith (9)
St Philip's CE Primary School, Bath

Snowman

S now is so great
N o one loves snow more than me
O h, I'm getting cold but I'm having too much fun
W ow, I won the snowball fight
M um, ten minutes more
A snowman, wow
N o one can stop me from playing in the snow.

Libby Walter (7)
St Philip's CE Primary School, Bath

Snowballs

S tay for longer in the snow
N o one can stop me from playing in the snow
O h no, here comes a snowball, leg it
W ant to build a snowman with me?
B y the time I come home from school the snow is gone
A little boy has fallen over in the snow
L ike my snowball
L akes filled with snow
S itting in the snow is so cold.

Abi Brewer (7)
St Philip's CE Primary School, Bath

Snow

S now falls like a soft feather drifting lightly
N obody doesn't like snow because it is beautiful
O h, snow is lovely
W hatever should I do without snow? I don't know
F luttering like fairies falling and falling
L ike shining stars in the sky
A very small fluffy cloud, the
K ey to the sky of snow
E ver and everlasting.

Maddie McCarthy (8)
St Philip's CE Primary School, Bath

Snowman

S now is drifting in my ear
N o one can stop me from playing in the snow
O h no, it's getting very windy
W ow, it's getting snowy
M elting snowflakes
A large cold flake dripping in my ear
N ow I can relax.

Aimee Huntley (7)
St Philip's CE Primary School, Bath

Snowman

S top throwing snowballs at me
N ow I've made a big snowball
O h, it's snowing today
W ow, look, snow
M any boys and girls throwing snowballs
A man has turned to ice
N ow there is lots of snow.

George Godwin (8)
St Philip's CE Primary School, Bath

Snowman

S now is coming today
N ever stops
O utside there is snow
W ow, the snow is here
M any snowmen outside
A snowman is cold
N ever stops snowing.

Ria Beeho (8)
St Philip's CE Primary School, Bath

Snowballs

S now is coming down
N ever stop snowing please
O h what a snowy day
W hat's that snow noise?
B alls are coming
A little snowman it is
L ittle snowballs are coming
L ittle white snowballs
S uper snow!

Jacob Quintin (8)
St Philip's CE Primary School, Bath

The Magic Box

(Based on 'Magic Box' by Kit Wright)

I will put in my box . . .
A white dragon with blue eyes
A bird with bright silver wings
And a magical thunder kingdom.

I will put in my box . . .
The three eyes of a golden alien
A hundred silvery blue crystals
And thousands of fine sweets.

I will put in my box . . .
A silver thunderbolt
A supercalafragalisticespialidocius chocolate bar
And an exotic fruit smoothie made from dragon nostrils.

My box is fashioned from ice, gold and steel
With moons on the lid and fireballs in the corners
Its hinges are made from golden stars.

I will fly in my box to Hawaii
To lie on the golden beach
Until I have to fly back home for tea.

Brandon Morrison (9)
St Philip's CE Primary School, Bath

Snowman

S now I love, let's go and play
N ever stop making snowmen
O h, I love snow
W ow, now let's have a snowball fight
M agnificent snowballs
A mazing dazzling ice
N ever forget falling snow.

Ben Bradley (8)
St Philip's CE Primary School, Bath

A Snowman

S now, snow, glorious snow, I could play in it all day
N o, snow is in my car
O h no, my cat is stuck in the snow
W ow, a big snowman in my front garden
B ig building with snow on top
A rgh, the snow is melting
L ook outside
L ovely soft snow.

Tallon Leach (8)
St Philip's CE Primary School, Bath

Snowman

S nowflakes falling from the sky
N ever stop playing in the snow
O pen up the curtains
W ow, many snowflakes are falling from the sky
M any people out in the snow
A nd never stop playing in it
N ever forget the falling snow.

Charlotte Marsh (8)
St Philip's CE Primary School, Bath

A Snowy Day

S nowball fight
N ever stop snowing
O h, it's snowing today
W ow, wow, the snow is falling
M any people in the snow
A snowman is growing
N ever go away.

Thomas Fowden (7)
St Philip's CE Primary School, Bath

Snowman

S loppy snow on the ground
N ever stop snowing, I want you to stay
O h, I love the snow, I love it so much
W hy do you fall on the ground?
M any snowballs falling, it is cold
A nd I must make a snowman, I must
N early going, I want you to stay.

Jess Szafran (8)
St Philip's CE Primary School, Bath

Snowman

S omething is falling fast
N ever stop snowing
O h, who wants a snowball fight?
W hoa, stop hitting my face with snowballs, Dad
M an, the snow is magic
A nd stop hitting the bus and driver
N ever stop snowing, please.

Brioney Evans (8)
St Philip's CE Primary School, Bath

Snow

S omething is falling from the sky
N ever stop waiting for the snow
O h no, the snow has gone
W ow, wow, it has come back again.

Sadie Moyle (8)
St Philip's CE Primary School, Bath

Snowman

S now is falling down from the sky
N ever stop building snowmen
O h, never ever stop snowing, oh never, oh never
W onderful snowflakes floating down from the sky
M any different hats and scarves
A wall full of icicles
N ever stop snowing, oh never, oh never.

Carla Ferris (8)
St Philip's CE Primary School, Bath

Snowballs

S now is the best
N o one can stop me
O h, snowballs are fun
W onderful snow
B ath is the best place for snow
A lways throw snowballs
L ots of snow
L ots of snowballs
S now is like bowling balls.

Curtis Gay (9)
St Philip's CE Primary School, Bath

Snow

S now, snow, here it comes
N o, no, don't go
O h, let's play in the snow
W hy it's gone, never mind.

Nick Atwell (8)
St Philip's CE Primary School, Bath

Snowman

S now, snow, I love the snow
N o one knows what it's made of
O h, what a wonderful sight
W ow, look outside and look how fast the snow falls
M any people love the snow but I love it the best
A snowball fight is really fun come and join everyone
N ever stop having a snowball fight because everyone knows
   that snow is the best.

Lucy Cryer (7)
St Philip's CE Primary School, Bath

Snowflake Adventure

S nowmen making is the tenth best thing
N o one is a snowman
O h, what a wonderful day
W hat a silly snowflake

A snow adventure is the best adventure
D on't stop snow fighting
V ery good snow
E xpress snow fight
N ever stop snow
T he best adventure
U nless white snow
R otten snowy leaves
E very snowy day.

Akhilesh Pai (9)
St Philip's CE Primary School, Bath

Snow Everywhere

S omething is falling
N ever stopping
O ut of the sky
W here did it come? Nobody knows

E veryone knows, what it is but I don't
V ery, very lightly, now as it comes
E choing splats falling on my tongue
R ising from the sky
Y ippee, I know where it comes from
W hat is it though?
H ere, I know, it's snow
E verywhere
R ound me and under me. Crunching under my welly boots
E verywhere it can be seen.

Karli-Anne Lunt (8)
St Philip's CE Primary School, Bath

Snowman

S omething is falling, snow
N ever stop throwing snow
O h, wonderful snow
W ow, what a sight of snow
M uch snow is melting
A crooked man is walking in the snow
N othing better than snow.

Sam Woodham (8)
St Philip's CE Primary School, Bath

Snowman

S omething is standing in my back garden
N ever know what it might be
O h, I know, it's a snowman
W ow, it looks cold
M aybe a hat and a scarf will make him warm
A nd some gloves
N ow he is nice and warm.

Jessica Bush (9)
St Philip's CE Primary School, Bath

Snowman

S o the snowman is white
N ever stop playing with snow
O h the snowman is big
W ow, I like snow
M any flakes are falling
A nd my dad is frozen
N ever forget the snow.

Wilson Skyrme (8)
St Philip's CE Primary School, Bath

Snowman

S now never stops falling
N ever eat snow
O h look, it's snowing
W ow, look at the snow
M y house is a snowball
A nd it's cold
N ever stop throwing snowballs.

Ellen Ascott (8)
St Philip's CE Primary School, Bath

Holocaust Memorial Day: Confusion

People are suffering, dying
What are they doing?
What shall I do?
What can I do?
I'm squashed, I'm cold
Where am I going?
Stop pulling me
People with shaved hair look ill
Inside my heart is breaking
And I can't stop it
I'm getting pulled
But I don't know where
People in lines
Wearing striped clothes
One day it's over
Why? They ask
No one knows.

Isabel Smith (9)
St Thomas a Becket School, Tilshead

Thoughts On Epiphany: The Three Kings

Plodding all day long
Sitting on the camels
By day we go through sandstorms
Bringing gold, myrrh and frankincense
Wearing rich purples and blues
Finally we arrive at the stable
All of us give our gifts
Now we leave the stable
Plodding all day long again.

Kiera O'Neill (10)
St Thomas a Becket School, Tilshead

Thoughts On Epiphany: Melchior

I am Melchior
Plodding on the hot scorching sand
The new king awaits
My stallion is tired and exhausted with aching legs
The gift I bring is frankincense, rich, dark and precious
My silky purple cloak gleams in the sun.

At last I arrive
My journey ends
My present to Jesus is well received
A blanket I also leave - rich in colours
As his life will be.

Tara Skinner (10)
St Thomas a Becket School, Tilshead

Holocaust Memorial Day: The Camp

I hate it here
I travelled in a cattle truck
To this concentration camp
My shoes go into a pile
I wear the Star of David
Going skinny, getting cold
When will I get out?
I said goodbye to my family
I feel down in the dumps
And now I feel I'm falling down
Going down, down underground
Oh why me?
Help me please!

Chloe Jackson (9)
St Thomas a Becket School, Tilshead

Thoughts On Epiphany: Travelling Magi

The Magi travelled through the scorching heat and freezing nights
Through the stinging sandstorms the camels plodded along
The Magi travelling in rich purple carrying gold, frankincense and myrrh
Going up and down the sand dunes, Melchior, Casper and Balthasar
Carrying Persian rugs, sitting on ornate saddles with tasselled bridles
Travelling in the twinkling night, stars gleaming
Moon shining, baby Jesus lies in a tatty stable.

Oliver Cogbill (9)
St Thomas a Becket School, Tilshead

Thoughts On Epiphany: The Three Kings

A glistening star takes us to a baby King
Our camels' feet brush on the cold sand
Horrible fierce sandstorms swoop into our faces
We sleep on the silky smooth sand
Our cloaks are made of rich yellows and purples
The twinkling moon shines bright above our heads
Tassels hang down from our loose robes
We wear strong beige turbans around our heads.

We come to a small tatty town
We see a wrecked and creaking stable
In the stable we found . . . the King
We lay three precious gifts before Him
Gold, frankincense and myrrh.

Ricky Lawrence (9)
St Thomas a Becket School, Tilshead

Thoughts On Epiphany: The Journey

The journey is long
And ever so tiring
But we have to go on.

Many miles we have travelled
Taking gifts to a Baby Boy
He's a King.

Gold, myrrh, frankincense
In glittering boxes
Gifts for Him.

Nearly there now
The stable is in sight
The Baby King in a crib
Sleeps as we leave gifts for Him.

Kyra Player (9)
St Thomas a Becket School, Tilshead

The Magic Of Christmas

It's Christmas Eve, I can't sleep
A bubbling, happy, jolly feeling inside me.

Waking the next morning
Hearing paper tearing
The noise of crackers popping
And the lovely sparkly fire.

Lunch smells of warm gravy and turkey
And tasty Brussels sprouts
Cranberry sauce and roast potatoes
I know it will all melt in my mouth.

Harriet Shakerley (10)
St Thomas a Becket School, Tilshead

Thoughts At Epiphany: The Three Wise Men

Camels plunge their feet into the scorching sand
Night brings twinkling stars and a gleaming moon
I feel a sandstorm coming
But our journey is nearly at an end
We shall find the special boy
We bring our gifts,
Gold, myrrh and frankincense
There is a stable up ahead
Inside a baby who will be King.

Iona Wilkinson (9)
St Thomas a Becket School, Tilshead

The Magic Of Christmas

I open my eyes
And I look around
I see decorations and my mini tree
I look at the clock
Oh no!
I'm up too early
I burst out of bed
Christmas!
I open my stocking
Sweets
I feel jolly
I feel fizzy
Come on!
Down the stairs
My toes are tingling
In the room
Lights, crackers, tree
And presents for me!

Daniel Evans (10)
St Thomas a Becket School, Tilshead

The Magic Of Christmas

In the magic of Christmas I hear:
Christmas crackers pulling
Christmas paper tearing
And the sound of a crackling fire.

In the magic of Christmas I can smell:
Sausages wrapped in bacon
Turkey in the oven
And candles flickering on the table.

In the magic of Christmas I see:
Happiness in my mum's face
Colours everywhere under the tree
And my pets eating their treats.

In the magic of Christmas I feel:
As if I'm going to pop
I whizz and fizz
Amazed at my presents.

This is my magical Christmas!

David Martin (10)
St Thomas a Becket School, Tilshead

Thoughts On Epiphany

E vening is coming, my journey is still long but I bring
P recious gold
I saw the comet gleaming bright
P assing the stars which sit at night
H igh above them is the most wondrous of all
A s I arrive the Baby awaits
N ow I give them the gift
Y ell to the world, 'The new King is here.'

Jake Atfield (9)
St Thomas a Becket School, Tilshead

The Magic Of Christmas

Waking up at 2am
Gifts on the bed
Excitement
I won't sleep again
Awake
Waiting
Fizzing with tension
The clock ticks unbearably slowly
3am
4am
Hours seem like days
5am
6am
The night never ends
6.15
6.30
Thirty minutes left
I see the presents
I can't control the excitement
6.45
Nearly there
Almost exploding now
6.59
Counting the seconds
5, 4, 3, 2, 1 . . .
It's Christmas!

Ruby Withers (11)
St Thomas a Becket School, Tilshead

Thoughts On Epiphany: Wise Men's Journey

Wise men walking
Camels plodding
And a star twinkling.

Sandstorms twirling
Sun boiling
And the moon shining.

Clothes gleaming
Purples glistening
And sand as golden as the sun.

Gold gleaming
Myrrh spicy
And frankincense fragrant.

Stable broken
Baby King screaming
But proud parents beaming.

Here at last!

Bradley Kinsey (11)
St Thomas a Becket School, Tilshead

The Magic Of Christmas

'It's Christmas, it's Christmas,' I cry.
'Wake up Mum, wake up!'
I feel so excited
I think I could burst any minute!
Brightly coloured paper all over my sister's floor
I open my gifts
I see the book I wanted and lots more
Later it's dinner
Smells of turkey, sausages and vegetables
I hear crackers
I see smiles
And that is the magic of Christmas.

Emily Withers (8)
St Thomas a Becket School, Tilshead

Holocaust Memorial Day

Watching people suffer
Blaming all the Jews
They think it doesn't matter about equal rights
So they give them abuse
Make the people work for them
Hate them day by day
Give them little food and watch them waste away.

Take their treasured possessions
Then put them in a pile
Give them beds three bunks high
And watch them cry and cry
Make them wear the Star of David
The end of their time is near
Treat them cruelly in the camps
And they'll not last a year.

What they did to them makes me cry
Why leave innocent people to die?
Well, I guess I'll never understand
Why Jewish people were left with no one to hold their hand.

Jessica Vincent (10)
St Thomas a Becket School, Tilshead

Holocaust Memorial Day: Last Stand

Pulled away in cattle trucks
We came to this horrible place
No one likes it here
They threw away our suitcases
We're afraid we will die here
We try to make a statement
We suffer
We get ill
So sad and so lonely
And we have little food
But no one wants to listen to us
So we remain here still.

Reuben Wright (9)
St Thomas a Becket School, Tilshead

Holocaust Memorial Day: A Jew

Distant memories of peace trouble my mind
Leaving everyone and everything behind
The only thing we have in common is our Star
But together we travel in cattle cars
Where we are going we do not know
Spirits and hopes for peace are low.

'Out, out,' shouts a distant voice
The Nazi waits with his rifle poised.
'Where are we?' we all cry
And I fear that this will be the place we'll die.

The smell courses through my nose
Morale is at an all time low
Stripped of my possessions, I have nothing
Even separated from those I love
Living in a draughty barracks with two men sleeping above.

Eventually, strange men taking me,
'Where am I going?' I plead
A man murmurs, 'Go,'
What happens next I do not know.

George Smith (10)
St Thomas a Becket School, Tilshead

Holocaust Memorial Day: My Thoughts

Hitler killing lots of Jews
Over thousands and thousands
Little babies and children too
Carts to transport Jews to the camps
Armies of gunmen with guns ready to shoot
Unbearable to lie in the camps
Sleeping on really uncomfortable beds
Little food or water
But trying to survive a couple more weeks or days.

Emma Miller (10)
St Thomas a Becket School, Tilshead

The Magic Of Christmas

The bang of crackers
Aromas of dinner scenting the house
Joyful people jumping
Pine needles spiking everyone who brushes past
Smiles on everyone's faces
Excited present-opening spree
Crackling of wrapping paper
Sparkling tinsel
Flickering candles
And tree lights glittering
Happiness tingles in tummies
Magical Christmas!

Luke Haggaty (8)
St Thomas a Becket School, Tilshead

Through That Door

Through that door
Is a crazy land of animals
Where crocodiles dance on the crazy river
And monkeys wearing ballet shoes and pink little tutus
Dancing around the fireplace singing la-la to the music.

Through that door
Is a cold and freezing jungle
Where polar bears live in the snow
And they roll and roll in the soft snow and smash the ice.

Through that door
Is a sandcastle
Where dolphins live and sit in the Jacuzzi
And do clever magic tricks.

Through that door
Is a land of jelly
You can always bounce every second and minute
Where jelly babies bounce in the fresh strawberry air.

Chiara Thiella (7)
West Coker Primary School, Yeovil

Through That Door

Through that door
Is a land of never-ending sweets
Children eat chocolate and sweets
Every day and night you can see
Children flying about like fairies
All children eat jelly babies for lunch, breakfast, tea.

Through that door
Is a crazy land of animals
Hippos fly around like fairies with wings
Multicoloured birds sit on swings and go over the bars
Crocodiles are ice skating around.

Through that door
Is a magical war
Where witches and angels battle for freedom
And dogs fight against cats.

Through that door
Is a funky disco where monkeys have their tea
And dance like elephants.

Lucy Manly (7)
West Coker Primary School, Yeovil

Through That Door

Through that door
Is a magic jelly bean land
Where giant jelly beans dance around
And where jelly beans fight jelly beans.

Through that door
Is a ghost town where skeletons tell jokes
And a treasure chest holds jelly beans.

Through that door
Is a magical land where fish climb trees
And elephants jump off swings and roundabouts.

Josh Boon (9)
West Coker Primary School, Yeovil

Through That Door

Through that door
Is a nice Jacuzzi with some naughty monkeys swimming
And seven worms drowning in the water
And a dog paddling.

Through that door
Is a magical animal land
Where the rhinos in the distance are flying
And birds go fishing for tea
And the fish have their tea.

Through that door
Is a land of wizards and witches
Their castles are gloomy and dark
Their cats and toads are scary
They are all freaky.

Nea Graziano (8)
West Coker Primary School, Yeovil

Through That Door

Through that door
Is a magic land of animals
Where fish have afternoon tea
And elephants dance like fairies
You can see beautiful lions flying high.

Through that door
Is a crazy farm
Where ducks sing the duck song
And the pigs have afternoon tea
When hens dance.

Through that door
Is a mermaid sitting on a rock
Singing to her best friends
To her favourite whale and sea lion
And then they go to the water park.

Emily Andrews (8)
West Coker Primary School, Yeovil

Through That Door

Through that door, through that door
Sniff, sniff
Lick your lips
I can see Georgia's tea with jumping beans.

Through that door, through that door
Sniff, sniff
Lick your lips
I can see a shopping spree
With my purse waiting for me.

Through that door, through that door
Sniff, sniff
Lick your lips
I can see my mum cooking for me
We are having stew.

Through that door, through that door
Sniff, sniff
Lick your lips
I can see Winston, Marie and Kammy
Playing in the fields.

Kim Centamore (9)
West Coker Primary School, Yeovil

Stress

Stress is a burgundy red
Stress feels light
Stress tastes like sour lemons
Stress sounds like thunder
Stress looks like a black cloud.

Bran Pick (10)
West Coker Primary School, Yeovil

Through That Door

Through that door
Is a magical war
Witches and wizards
Toads and lizards
Where the lions lie
The elephants fly
Chickens are chickens
When the owls howl and take flight
Through the winter's night.

Through that door
Is a psychedelic land
And it stands up straight
And its weight is over 2,000,000 tons
Ghosts live there
The only thing they eat are pears
They always have a pair of skirts to wear.

Charlie Cowley (8)
West Coker Primary School, Yeovil

Love

Love is red
Love is chocolate
Love is joy
Love is smiles
Love is cuddles
Love is kisses
Love is roses
Love is excitement
Love is happy
Love is hearts
And most of all
Love is together forever.

Francesca Graziano (10)
West Coker Primary School, Yeovil

Through That Door

Through that door
Is a magic land for animals
Where cats play day and night
And dogs chew their bones all day, every day.

Through that door
Is a big shopping mall
Where elephants are singing
And goldfish are dancing.

Through that door
Are people dancing with cows
When horses are running around
And pigs are flying.

Through that door
Is a magic place for love
Where people are holding hands
And kissing on the cheek.

Charlotte Taylor (8)
West Coker Primary School, Yeovil

Love

Love is like a sweet-smelling rose
Love is like a soft-sounding melody
Love is like a heart-shaped balloon

L ove is like delicious hot chocolate
O range, red and pink are the colours of love
V alentine's Day symbolises love
E veryone deserves love

Love symbolises together forever.

Victoria White (9)
West Coker Primary School, Yeovil

Through That Door

Through that door
Is a magical war
Where witches and angels battle for freedom
And dogs eat ketchup
And chickens are dumb
And chicks are dumb in a magic world.

Through that door
Is a cook burning a can of frogs
And worms wriggling in a bowl of stew
When the cooker cooked a frog
It normally blew up in the world of frogs.

Through that door
Is a football world where Arsenal always win
And Manchester United lose every day
And Concorde flies for Arsenal
And the crowd jumps on the football pitch.

Danny Gilham (8)
West Coker Primary School, Yeovil

Happiness

Happiness is a yellow sun beaming over the Earth
Happiness is a golden crown sitting on the Queen's head
Happiness is snuggling down on the sofa watching a DVD
Happiness is a huge Galaxy chocolate bar
Happiness is eating an ice cream on a hot summer's day
Happiness is having a lie-in on a Saturday morning
Happiness is opening presents at Christmas
And most of all happiness is spending time with your family.

Molly Morris (10)
West Coker Primary School, Yeovil

Through That Door

Through that door
Is a magic land of animals
Where fish have afternoon tea
And elephants dance like fairies
You can see beautiful lions flying high
And multicoloured birds playing on roller-skates in the park
And a lovely, beautiful, peaceful garden.

Through that door
Is a romantic underground palace
Where elephants are playing in the water
They have afternoon tea
And a bit later they play chess
Then they play on their roller-skates in the park
With flowers floating peacefully in the garden
With lovely, peaceful, green grass.

Sophie Pinkett (8)
West Coker Primary School, Yeovil

Through That Door

Through that door
Is a magic land of animals
Where fish have Tuesday tea
And elephants dance like fairies
Penguins flying high
Coloured birds playing in the garden.

Through that door
Is a sweet land that is made of blue sweets
A pink queen dancing in the sweet castle
Then the sweet penguins swimming in the sweet sea.

Joshua Cresswell (8)
West Coker Primary School, Yeovil

Through That Door

Through that door
Is a magical wood of animals
Where mad tigers drive pink and purple cars
And squirrels climb up high trees
And woodpeckers are pecking at the trees.

Through that door
Is a palace named Buckingham Palace
Where servants are making breakfast for the Queen
Stupid guests on skateboards
And children picking their noses.

Through that door
Is a football pitch packed with fans
Where people are cheering for their team when they score
People waiting for the full-time whistle to blow because their
team are winning.

Henry Morris (8)
West Coker Primary School, Yeovil

Through That Door

Through that door
Is a green jungle of cats
Cats dancing in the sun
Cats sleeping in the golden sun
Cats having afternoon tea.

Through that door
Is a deep blue sea
Where a dolphin is dancing in the waves
Sharks watch a movie at the cinema
Fish eat whale.

Through that door
Is a secret island
Where unicorns fly from tree to tree
Birds digging their way underground.

Otis Pick (8)
West Coker Primary School, Yeovil

Through That Door

Through that door
Is a secret enchanted garden
Where flowers grow wild
The lions glide through the air
And dogs live underground.

Through that door
Is a beautiful vision of space
Where stars have fun playing on roller skates
The moon is having a game of football.

Through that door
Is a beautiful underwater sea waiting to be discovered
With dancing and prancing sharks singing
And hundreds of dolphins doing back and front flips
Fish having afternoon tea.

Sammy Hubbard (7)
West Coker Primary School, Yeovil

Love

Love is red like a star falling from the sky
Love is pink like a rose growing in the garden
Love is blue like the sea sparkling in the sun.

Jenny Taylor (10)
West Coker Primary School, Yeovil

Love

Love is . . .
Sweet chewy chocolate
Bouncy, pink, heart-shaped balloons
Slow-rhyming love songs
The fresh scent of roses
Lovely cuddly hugs.

Megan Manly (9)
West Coker Primary School, Yeovil

Friendship

F riends always look out for each other
R eally good friends are the best people to be with
I mportant to have friends
E njoy your time with your friends
N o people are not your friends
D o you have lots of friends?
S hould you be a better friend?
H ow many friends have you got?
I s your friend the best friend ever?
P eople all over the world have friends.

Jake Symes (9)
West Coker Primary School, Yeovil

Happiness

The happy times we have together
The sun always shines bright
The family walks and swims
The sun smiles down at us
When we are happy and others are we will know
Because the sun will be shining down on us
Yellow as the sun is happiness.

Bethany Hubbard (10)
West Coker Primary School, Yeovil

Anger

Anger is red like boiling hot water
It feels like a volcano is erupting inside you
Anger is like a red-hot fire
It feels hot, jagged and spiky.

Jemma Reddaway (10)
West Coker Primary School, Yeovil

Young Writers Information

We hope you have enjoyed reading this
book - and that you will continue to enjoy it
in the coming years.

If you like reading and writing poetry drop
us a line, or give us a call, and we'll send
you a free information pack.

Alternatively if you would like to order
further copies of this book or any of our
other titles, then please give us a call or
log onto our website at
www.youngwriters.co.uk

Young Writers Information
Remus House
Coltsfoot Drive
Peterborough
PE2 9JX
(01733) 890066